W9-CBC-931

Stuff Every

AMERICAN

Should Know

Library of Congress Cataloging in Publication Number: 2011946050

ISBN: 978-1-59474-582-9

Printed in China

Typeset in Monotype Old Style and Goudy

Designed by Katie Hatz
Production management by John J. McGurk

Quirk Books
215 Church Street
Philadelphia, PA 19106
quirkbooks.com

Stuff Every

AMERICAN

Should Know

By Denise Kiernan and Joseph D'Agnese

QUIRK BOOKS
PHILADELPHIA

Introduction

There are certain things every American should know and others you can probably let slide. The names of all the presidents in the order in which they served? Maybe not.

The lyrics to the first stanza of "The Star-Spangled Banner"? Absolutely.

This book, which purports to be about stuff every American should know, is admittedly selective, idiosyncratic, and likely to touch off arguments. "Why did they spend all that time talking about Pilgrims and leave out Mickey Mantle?" someone is bound to ask. Why? Because we're citizens of a democratic republic that values freedom, that's why! Welcome to America.

You see, people of other nations define themselves by their race, religion, ethnicity, or shared cultural heritage. America, a nation of immigrants, defines itself by its beliefs, the biggest of which is enshrined in the Declaration of Independence: *all men are created equal*. You think someone in Europe could come up with this stuff? Okay, actually, that concept grew out of ideas espoused in the Enlightenment, an intellectual movement that began in eighteenth-century Europe. But hey, hot dogs, football, apple pie, and rockin' country music are now all totally American, too, even if they originated outside the good ole U.S. of A.

This book is about all those little things you probably never got around to asking your social studies teacher. What did they eat at the first Thanksgiving? What's the electoral college? What books changed America? Is it true you're breaking the law if you rip a dollar bill?

The answers to these questions—whether political, cultural, trivial, or ridiculous—are things you probably ought to know if you want to feel truly patriotic and impress your family and friends on the next Fourth of July.

So gather around, wrap yourself in Old Glory, and get ready to dig into some essential stuff about the greatest country on the planet.

Where did America get its name?

You'd think our continent would be called North Columbus. After all, when Europeans were boldly drawing maps and naming giant swaths of land, Christopher Columbus was the explorer most closely associated with travels to the far side of the Atlantic.

But instead, America was named after the mysterious Florentine explorer Amerigo Vespucci. He may have made as many as four voyages to the New World, although two are disputed by historians. In letters describing his journeys, Vespucci asserted that the newly discovered land was *not* part of Asia but rather a new continent he dubbed the "New World"—an idea and phrase that Columbus never put forward.

In 1507, a German cartographer named Martin Waldseemüller printed the first map featuring the word *America*. "I can see no reason why anyone would . . . object to calling this . . . after the man of great ability who discovered it," wrote Waldseemüller, apparently under the false impression that Vespucci's travels preceded those of Columbus. In the centuries that followed, many would paint Vespucci as a huckster who schemed his way into history. Ralph Waldo Emerson said with disdain, "Strange that broad America must wear the name of a thief! Amerigo Vespucci . . . managed in this lying world to supplant Columbus, and baptize half the earth with his own dishonest name!"

In truth, Vespucci probably did nothing dishonest. Modern historians believe Waldseemüller was led astray by salacious forged documents printed by scamming publishers that made it seem like Vespucci beat Columbus to these shores. When Waldseemüller learned of his mistake, he revised the map so the continent was labeled "Terra incognita" (unknown land).

But the first name stuck. In 2003, the Library of Congress spent $10 million for the only surviving version of Waldseemüller's America map, now on display in Washington D.C.

What's the difference between the Declaration of Independence and the U.S. Constitution?

You'd be surprised how many people mix these up. Everyone from presidents to political pundits have referenced the wrong documents in their speeches. The differences are vast and important. Let's take a look.

The Declaration of Independence . . .

. . . is about 1,300 words long.

. . . begins with: "When in the course of human events . . ."

. . . separated the 13 original colonies from the control of Great Britain.

. . . does not govern the American people (though its ideals, notably the concept of "life, liberty, and the pursuit of happiness," are embraced by citizens as an expression of quintessentially American values).

. . . was signed by 56 men beginning on August 2, 1776, and possibly not signed by the last signer until 1781.

The U.S. Constitution . . .

. . . is about 7,500 words long, including 27 amendments.

. . . begins with the words "We the People . . ."

. . . governs Americans and provides for the executive, legislative, and judicial branches of government.

. . . is the document that presidents, soldiers, government officials, and new American citizens must swear to uphold and protect.

. . . was signed by 39 men on September 17, 1787, and later ratified or accepted by all 13 states.

Who invented blue jeans?

The answer, surprisingly, is *not* Levi Strauss, though he certainly helped popularize them in the United States. Before this all-American garment became popular in the Wild West, variations were being sold in other parts of the world. In the sixteenth century, merchants in Bombay, India, sold a hard-wearing blue fabric out of the Dongari Fort that was dubbed *dungaree*. In the port town of Genoa, Italy, sailors used a similar fabric to make sails, tarps, and clothing. And the city of Nîmes, France—about 300 miles from Genoa along the French–Italian Riviera—was home to a factory that produced *serge de Nîmes*, from which comes the English word *denim*. The French spoke of the Italian fabric as the "blue of Genoa" (*bleu de Gênes*), hence *blue jeans* in English.

Denim was an ideal choice for working-class clothing. It was remarkably durable, concealed stains, and became more comfortable with use. In 1853, at the time of the California gold rush, a German dry-goods merchant named Levi Strauss opened a business in San Francisco, intending to sell supplies to miners. Strauss teamed up with a Nevada tailor, Jacob Davis, to create pants that stood up to the punishing grind of mining work. When customers complained that the pockets and other parts of the pants tore too easily, Strauss and Davis strengthened the stress points of the garment with copper rivets. They received a U.S. patent for this design in 1873. A rivet placed in the crotch was later dropped from the design because it conducted heat to sensitive parts of the body when wearers squatted in front of campfires.

Ten Great Architectural Wonders in America

E ven people who don't give a hoot about architecture grow quiet when they stare out across the reflecting pool toward the Lincoln Memorial. There are hundreds of buildings, structures, and sites in the United States that inspire awe. Here are ten you'll want to explore in person.

1. **Mesa Verde (c. 1190)**

   When they migrated south in 1300, the Anasazi people of Colorado left behind a massive city built of sandstone and adobe under a cliff. Considered the best-preserved example of cliff dwellings in the world, the site is now a national park that attracts about 500,000 visitors annually.

2. **Monticello (1770)**

   Brilliant, artistic Thomas Jefferson designed this mountaintop house in Virginia. Visitors enjoy inspecting his inventions, artwork, and farms as they prowl the 5,000-acre site.

3. **Biltmore Estate (1895)**

   Built by George W. Vanderbilt, a descendant of the seventh wealthiest family in history, this French chateau–style building is the largest private residence in the United States. Its 250 rooms include a bowling alley and an indoor swimming pool.

4. **The Empire State Building (1931)**
   Standing at 1,250 feet (without its spire), this art deco masterpiece is the tallest skyscraper in New York City since the loss of

the World Trade Center in 2001. It also boasts the famous climb of King Kong.

5. **Fallingwater (1938)**

Only an architect as bold as Frank Lloyd Wright would have dared to build a home over a waterfall. Now open to the public, this Bear Run, Pennsylvania, home welcomes 150,000 visitors annually.

6. **Verrazano-Narrows Bridge (1964)**

Though not as beautiful as the gothic Brooklyn Bridge or as colorful as the bright orange Golden Gate Bridge, this 4,260-foot-long span linking Brooklyn and Staten Island is the longest bridge in the United States. The Golden Gate is second, at 4,200 feet.

7. **Gateway Arch (1965)**

This gleaming, 630-foot stainless steel arch is a symbol of St. Louis's position as the gateway to the American West.

Visitors can take the stairs or ride to the top in a tram or elevator.

8. **World Trade Center (1972)**

   The Twin Towers were the tallest and most visible buildings attacked by terrorists on September 11, 2001, but five other buildings in the complex were also destroyed that day. The site is now home to the National September 11 Memorial and Museum. A commercial building informally known as the Freedom Tower is slated for completion in 2013. At 1,776 feet, it will be the tallest building in the United States.

9. **The Willis Tower (1973)**

   At 1,450 feet to its roof, this Chicago structure is currently the tallest in the United States. In 2009, three glass balconies were added to its Skydeck, allowing visitors to step out and look down to the street below.

10. Vietnam Veterans Memorial (1982)

When Maya Lin's controversial black-granite design was first unveiled, many Americans considered it bland and unassuming. But it soon became a pilgrimage site for families of veterans and an emotional touchstone for all Americans.

What's the difference between a Pilgrim and a Puritan?

The difference is small but significant. Remember the Reformation, when people broke away from the Roman Catholic church and spun off a new religion called Protestantism? The Church of England grew out of that famous split, but some people didn't think it went far enough. These folks viewed the Anglican church—with its fancy robes and ritualized tradition—as just another version of what they considered to be the corrupted and decadent Catholic church. These protestors, called Puritans, wanted to further purify the English church.

The Puritans were split into two factions: Separatists and non-Separatists. Separatists wanted to break entirely from the Church of England and start their own church. The non-Separatists didn't want to split; they valued a connection to the existing church and longed for a modification of its views. Disgruntled, a group of Separatist Puritans left England, setting out first for Holland and then the New World. On their journey to their new home, aboard a little vessel known as the *Mayflower*, these die-hards referred to themselves as pilgrims. They settled in Plymouth Plantation and became closely identified with the Thanksgiving holiday that Americans celebrate today.

Ten years later, as anti-Puritan sentiment grew in England, their non-Separatist brethren, the Puritans, fled to America and founded the Massachusetts Bay Colony and the city of Boston. These more prosperous and more zealous Puritans live on in popular culture as the ornery group who burned witches and made people wear scarlet letters.

What was served at the First Thanksgiving?

The Pilgrims landed in 1620 and suffered a miserable winter in their new home; nearly half died. The next fall brought a bountiful harvest, and the settlers celebrated with a feast held on December 13, 1621. However, there's no documentation to suggest that turkey was the focus of the meal. Instead, food historians believe that the Pilgrims feasted on edibles then abundant in Plymouth colony: oysters, eels, geese, corn, leeks, venison, and berries. Journal entries from that year mention everything from bass and cod to deer and, yes, wild turkeys, so it is possible the bird was on the menu, too. Two years later, in 1623, cranberries and pumpkin pie were added to the feast.

How to Carve a Turkey

Sure, it'd be nice to slice up that giant gobbler in front of the entire family. But top chefs agree that the best way to carve a big bird is to dismember it in your kitchen and present guests with an artfully arranged platter of meat that can be easily served at the table. Working out of sight allows you to enlist the aid of some tools you probably won't want to use in front of company, namely, your hands. Here's how it's done:

1. **Let the bird rest.** Don't even think about carving the turkey until it has been out of the oven for 20 to 30 minutes. During cooking, moisture is driven toward the outer layers of the bird. Resting allows the juices to sink back in.

2. **Remove the legs.** Use a knife to cut the skin attaching each of the legs to the breast. Then bend the legs down until the hip joints pop. They should come loose easily, but you can work a carving knife into the joints to finish the job if needed. Cut the meat around the leg and remove each one from the bird. Set the legs on a cutting board. Using your fingers and a carving knife, feel around for the joints connecting the thighbone to the drumsticks. Upon cutting them, you will have two thighs and two drumsticks. Place these on your serving platter, skin side up. (If the turkey is especially large, you may wish to strip the meat from the bones and carve it into smaller slices.)

3. **Remove the wings.** Lift the wings away from the breast, slice the skin, and work your knife into the wing joints until they are severed. Remove the wings, along with

surrounding dark meat. Place the wings on your platter, skin side up.

4. **Remove the stuffing.** Place the stuffing in bowls that can be easily passed around and shared. Otherwise you're forcing your guests to participate in an ungainly mining expedition.

5. **Carve the breast.** You'll be left with a large portion of breast meat still on the bone. Slice across the top of the bird and remove half the breast meat in one large section. Place it skin side up on a carving board, hold it steady, and neatly carve skin and meat into thin slices. Repeat with the other breast. Carefully arrange the white meat slices on the platter with the dark meat. Whisk the platter out to your hungry guests.

6. **Deal with the carcass and leftovers later.** Carving this way allows you to easily store leftovers in plastic containers without

having to find room for the carcass in your refrigerator. By the way, the carcass can be boiled for soup stock—or fed to ravenous uncles who have nothing better to do than scavenge the remaining bits of meat from the bones.

Ten Foods Invented in America

Pizza may be the most delicious food on the planet, but it wasn't born in America. Nor were macaroni and cheese, fries, ice cream, or tacos. Here's a list of ten delicious treats that America *can* lay claim to.

1. **"Velvet" cake:** There are two main types. The chocolate velvet cake—a dense, fudgy wedge of chocolaty sin—was first created by pastry chef Albert Kumin when he was working at the Four Seasons restaurant in New York in 1959. The second type, the red velvet cake, is a festive dessert served by generations of gracious Southern hostesses. Despite stories of chefs using beets as a sugar substitute,

the red velvet cake most likely grew out of a depression-era marketing campaign for food dye. The color bestowed a regal quality to the chocolate or vanilla-flavored cake.

2. **Corn dog:** A frankfurter dipped in corn-meal batter and deep fried. What could be better? The resulting corn dog has an unclear provenance. A 1929 patent was awarded to Stanley Jenkins for a machine that allowed vendors to fry foods impaled on a stick, but around the same time other restaurant supply catalogs offered similar devices. Neil Fletcher of Texas is credited with having sold his "Original State Fair Corny Dogs" in 1942. Today, corn dogs are classic staples of American state fairs because they're festive, fun, and easy to carry and eat.

3. **Cheesesteak:** Passyunk Avenue in down-town Philadelphia is the epicenter of

cheesesteak lore. Pat and Henry Olivieri claim to have created the classic sandwich in the 1930s, grilling thinly sliced steak and serving it in a roll, either plain; with onions, mushrooms, peppers, and other toppings; or topped with provolone, American cheese, or Cheez Whiz. The sandwich is now found on menus nationwide.

4. **Chop suey and chow mein:** You'd be hard-pressed to find what passes for Chinese food in the United States on menus in China. Chop suey (meat and veggies) and chow mein (meat and veggies over fried noodles) were first devised beginning in the 1850s by Chinese or Chinese American chefs who served Chinese workers building railroads across the United States. By the turn of the 20th century, the dishes made the leap to Chinese restaurants frequented (tellingly) by American, not Chinese, diners.

5. **Waldorf, Cobb, and Caesar Salad:** The *Waldorf* salad—which adds chopped apples, walnuts, and celery to a salad tossed in mayo dressing—was first conceived by Oscar Tschirky, a clever maitre d' who worked at the Waldorf-Astoria hotel in New York. Tschirky may have included the salad in a recipe book he edited for the restaurant in 1896.

The *Cobb*—a salad made with turkey or chicken, diced hard-boiled eggs, avocado, bacon, scallions, and Roquefort cheese over greens —is believed to have originated at the Hollywood Brown Derby restaurant in the 1930s and been named after restaurateur Robert Cobb.

The *Caesar* is attributed to Caesar Cardini, an Italian immigrant who opened restaurants in San Diego and Tijuana, Mexico. His family claims that Cardini invented the salad—cheese and croutons tossed atop greens graced with a dressing of egg, lemon juice, and Worcestershire sauce—during a busy Fourth of July rush at his Tijuana location.

6. **Anadama bread:** An angry New England fisherman gets fed up with his wife's bread and concocts a dark loaf of his own consisting of cornmeal and molasses. "Anna, damn it, that's what I like," he says, and this bread with a strange name is born. Is the story, or its many variants, true? No one can say, but the sweet, chewy bread is tasty anyway.

7. **Oysters Bienville, Kirkpatrick, and Rockefeller:** No nation can claim to have invented the oyster, but these three dishes all originated in the United States. The creamy green pepper, onion, cheese, and breadcrumb Bienville dish is named after the founder of New Orleans and was invented by Antoine's, the city's famous restaurant, in the 1930s or '40s. The

Kirkpatrick green pepper and bacon preparation came to life at the Palace Hotel in San Francisco during the turn of the 20th century. The key ingredients of Oysters Rockefeller, also invented at Antoine's, may well be the best-kept secret in the world. (Its chef-creator insisted on his deathbed that the recipe remain a secret.) Restaurants throughout the world have developed their own versions of this mysterious green, creamy, anise-flavored dish.

8. **Buffalo chicken wings:** The scene is the Anchor bar, Buffalo, New York, 1964. Owner Teressa Bellissimo receives a larger-than-expected order of chicken wings and decides to serve them to her patrons with a spicy hot sauce. A napkin-consuming legend is born, which spreads far beyond the snowy home of the Bills.

9. **Spiedies:** Shoemaking Italian immigrants in Binghamton, New York, snapped up these local sandwiches from vendors as early as the 1930s. Marinated cubes of chicken, lamb, pork, or other meats were grilled on a skewer and then swiped off the stick with a slice of squishy white "Italian" bread. The skewer is tossed, and patrons eat the resulting sandwich. Now spiedies are enjoyed all across the United States, and not just by residents of "Bingoland."

10. **Toll House cookie:** When Ruth Wakefield first baked her now-famous "chocolate crunch cookie" at her historic Toll House Inn in Massachusetts in the 1930s, she broke up bars of Nestlé chocolate and tossed the tiny chunks into her batter. The chocolate melted slightly but remained fairly chunky. She allowed the Nestlé company to print the recipe on their chocolate bars, and soon the entire nation was baking

these distinctive "chocolate chip" cookies. It wasn't until 1939 that Nestlé started packaging droplike chips so that home cooks wouldn't have to chop bars into bits.

What does the Bill of Rights allow me to do?

The first ten amendments of the U.S. Constitution are known as the Bill of Rights. They were ratified (or accepted) by the states in 1791, shortly after the first Congress went into business. These days, whenever Americans argue about the Constitution, it seems that what they're really arguing about is the Bill of Rights. Here's what that document is all about.

The First Amendment: Freedom of Expression

This amendment includes the freedom of religion, speech, and the press. It gives people the right to assemble peaceably and to petition the government to address grievances.

The Second Amendment: The Right to Bear Arms

This amendment has always been controversial because the Founding Fathers prefaced the right by mentioning it in connection with militias. In colonial days, civilian men were expected to keep guns and be available to defend their communities as part of militias. The famous Minutemen belonged to a militia. In 2008, the Supreme Court ruled that this amendment did indeed give individuals not connected to a militia the right to keep guns.

The Third Amendment: The Quartering of Troops

Much of the resentment American colonists felt toward British troops grew out of being forced to pay for the soldiers' room and board or give up room in their homes to shelter them. We don't want these soldiers here, the colonists argued, so why should we be forced to house them? This amendment, which protects Americans from being forced to house troops during peacetime, has also been interpreted as granting Americans a right to privacy and recognizing that your home is your castle.

The Fourth Amendment: Unreasonable Searches and Seizures

Simply put, the government must issue a specific warrant before it can enter your home and search your belongings for evidence of a crime.

The Fifth Amendment: Due Process of Law

Yes, this amendment gives you "the right to remain silent," or, rather, the right not to be forced to bear witness against yourself. But it also says you can't be forced to stand trial for a crime unless a jury indicts you first; you can't be tried twice for the same crime; you can't be jailed, executed, or deprived of your property without due process of law; and the government can't seize your property for public use (building highways, parks, etc.) without compensating you fairly.

The Sixth Amendment: The Right to a Fair Trial

You have the right to a speedy and public trial by a jury of your peers. You have the right to know what you're being charged with, to confront the witnesses against you, to subpoena witnesses, and to have an attorney.

The Seventh Amendment: Trial by Jury in Civil Cases

The Founding Fathers certainly were serious about trial by jury because this is the third time they mention it in the Bill of Rights. This time, however, the right to have a jury extends to civil cases, those in which two people are suing each other. This amendment says judges cannot toss out the jury's verdict unless they follow specific procedures.

The Eighth Amendment: Cruel and Unusual Punishment

This amendment protects the rights of prisoners. They can't be hit with excessive bails or fines, and "cruel and unusual punishments" cannot be inflicted upon them. This last phrase remains controversial as Americans struggle with the constitutionality of executing people for their crimes.

The Ninth Amendment: Unenumerated Rights

This may not sound like the sexiest amendment, but it's a catchall. The framers were saying that people of the United States "retain" certain rights even if they are not spelled out in the Constitution. Over the years, this awkward phrasing has been taken to mean such things as the right to privacy, the right to go where you please, and so on. Some experts call it the "forgotten amendment."

The Tenth Amendment: States' Rights

This amendment says that any powers not delegated to the United States by the Constitution (or prohibited by the Constitution) are reserved to the States, or to the people.

Is it *really* illegal to rip a dollar bill in half?

Yes. Despite the prevalence of those penny stamping/squishing machines found in arcades and souvenir shops, it is technically illegal to do anything to a coin or paper currency that interferes with its ability to travel the world acting as a piece of legal tender. Defacement of U.S. currency violates Title 18, Section 333 of the U.S. Code, which reads: "Whoever mutilates, cuts, defaces, disfigures, or perforates, or unites or cements together, or does any other thing to any bank bill, draft, note, or other evidence of debt issued by any national banking association, or Federal Reserve bank, or the Federal Reserve System, with intent to render such bank bill, draft, note, or other evidence of debt unfit to be reissued, shall be fined under this title or imprisoned not more than six months, or both."

The Secret Service is responsible for enforcement. But before you flee the country for drawing a mustache on George Washington's face, understand that the law is lightly enforced in cases of small-time defacement. The law is really about altering bills or coins in such a way that they can't be used again. If you were to mutilate thousands of bills as part of an art installation, marketing scheme, or crafty project, you'd probably attract the attention of scary men in suits. But defacing that much currency is expensive, time-consuming, and illogical. You'd probably lose more money than the kicks would be worth.

Who played the first game of football?

Every American knows the basics of football. Teams advance across a gridiron to score touchdowns. There are huge goal posts. Players wear helmets and shoulder pads. There are field goals and interceptions and time-outs.

But if you time-traveled back to November 6, 1869, to watch what many call the first college football game, you'd immediately notice that it was nothing at all like the game you know and love. When teams from Rutgers and Princeton beat each other to a pulp that day on a field in New Brunswick, New Jersey, they were playing a game that more closely resembles soccer. Or rugby. And no one wore helmets. In fact, some players wore brightly colored turbans so their teammates could tell them apart from their opponents. By the way: Rutgers won, 6–4.

Rematches were hard to evaluate because every team had its own rules for how the game was played. When you played on their turf, you played by their rules. On some days, the game looked like soccer. On others, it was a scrappy variant of rugby. Either way, players went home bloodied. Or dead.

In the 1870s, organizers began meeting in Massachusetts to hammer out stricter rules because critics complained the game was too dangerous, and teams were having trouble convincing their universities to let them play. A frequent attendee and contributor at these rules talks was a young Yale student and football team captain named Walter Camp, now regarded as the father of American football. Camp purged all vestiges of rugby from the game and dreamed up an entirely new one, complete with new rules, field designs, and even a unique method of scoring. Football historians say the game really started in 1882, the day Camp imagined the gridiron, but there would be further innovations along the way.

According to the Football Hall of Fame, the first official pro game was played on November 12, 1892, when one player—William "Pudge" Heffelfinger—pocketed $500 to play for the Allegheny Athletics against the Pittsburgh Athletics. Allegheny won, 4–0.

Where did Mount Rushmore come from?

Obviously not a natural phenomenon, this famous sculpture high in the Black Hills of South Dakota was originally conceived as a way of drumming up tourist dollars for this sparsely populated state. More than 80 years later, the scheme is working: 2.3 million people visited the site in 2010.

In 1923, the state's official historian, Doane Robinson, dreamed up the idea of carving famous faces into a mountainside. He persuaded Gutzon Borglum, an American-born sculptor of Danish descent, to create it—Borglum chose the site, the design, and even the presidents. For 14 years, until his death in spring 1941, Borglum dynamited and shaped granite to form the 60-foot heads of George Washington, Thomas Jefferson, Theodore Roosevelt, and

Abraham Lincoln. His son, Lincoln Borglum, continued his father's work until funding fizzled later that year.

The sculpture as we know it is technically incomplete. The elder Borglum had originally intended to include Washington's torso and arm and a bit more of the other presidents' busts. Today the monument is operated by the U.S. National Park Service and is undoubtedly the most visited site in the state.

Assassinations of U.S. Presidents

Though there have been several assassination attempts on U.S. presidents throughout history, only four men have lost their lives to assassins while in office.

President: Abraham Lincoln (16th president)
Date attacked: April 14, 1865
What happened: John Wilkes Booth, an actor and Confederate sympathizer, gained access to the president's unguarded box at Ford's Theatre in Washington, D.C., during an evening production of *Our American Cousin*, shooting the president in the back of the head with a derringer. Lincoln was carried to a house across the street and died the next morning. Twelve days later, Booth was killed by soldiers after a federal manhunt

tracked him to a Virginia farmhouse. Andrew Johnson assumed the presidency.

President: James A. Garfield (20th president)
Date attacked: July 2, 1881
What happened: Upset that he did not receive appointments to various government posts (for which he was not qualified or even considered), Charles J. Guiteau, a delusional lawyer, used a .44 revolver to shoot Garfield on a train platform in Washington, D.C. The president languished for 11 weeks and finally died on September 19, 1881, at the New Jersey shore, where he'd been moved to take in the sea air. Some historians blame inept medical practices for his ultimate death. Guiteau was hanged. Chester Arthur assumed the presidency.

President: William McKinley (25th president)
Date attacked: September 16, 1901
What happened: Believing that he was acting on behalf of the common man, Leon Czolgosz,

a factory worker and anarchist, shot McKinley twice with a .32 revolver during the Pan-American Exposition in Buffalo, New York, as the president shook hands with a long line of citizens. One bullet grazed the president but did not enter his body. Doctors were unable to remove the other. The president appeared to recover but succumbed to shock and died from gangrene eight days later. Czolgosz was sentenced to the electric chair. Theodore Roosevelt assumed the presidency.

President: John F. Kennedy (35th president)
Date attacked: November 22, 1963
What happened: Kennedy was shot and killed while riding in an open limousine in Dealey Plaza on a visit to Dallas, Texas. A bolt-action rifle was found at the scene of a book depository where Lee Harvey Oswald, the presumed gunman, worked. When arrested, Oswald denied involvement; he was killed two days later by nightclub owner Jack Ruby while in police

custody. Though a government commission concluded that Oswald had acted alone, the assassination looms large in American culture as the mother of all conspiracies. Ruby died of cancer in prison. Lyndon B. Johnson assumed the presidency.

Foiled Assassinations of U.S. Presidents

Beginning with Andrew Jackson in 1835, presidents have been the targets of many assassination attempts. People have tried to shoot them (Jackson, Franklin D. Roosevelt, Harry Truman, Gerald Ford, Jimmy Carter, Bill Clinton, George H. W. and George W. Bush), bomb them (John F. Kennedy, George H. W. Bush, Clinton), lob grenades at them (George W. Bush), and fly planes into the White House (Richard Nixon, Bill Clinton). But in only two cases did an assassin's bullet penetrate the body of a president and *not* result in death.

Theodore Roosevelt: Sure, he was technically a former president when he was attacked in 1912, but the story is too remarkable to omit. After two terms in office, Roosevelt had handed the presidency to his protégé William Howard Taft in 1908. But he returned to the campaign trail four years later to pursue another term in the White House. While preparing to give a campaign speech in Milwaukee, Roosevelt was shot by a bartender named John Schrank; the bullet penetrated Roosevelt's clothing, eyeglass case, the text of his speech, and the surface of his skin, but went no further.

The savvy Roosevelt made the most of the opportunity and worked the assassination attempt into his 3,800-word address. "Friends, I shall ask you to be as quiet as possible," he began. "I don't know whether you fully understand that I have just been shot; but it takes more than that to kill a Bull Moose. But fortunately I had my manuscript, so you see I was going to make a long speech, and there is a bullet—there is where the bullet went through—and it probably saved me from it going into my heart. The bullet is in me now, so that I cannot make a very long speech, but I will try my best." Roosevelt declined to have doctors remove the bullet, which he carried to his grave seven years later. The deranged Schrank spent the rest of his life in a mental institution.

Ronald Reagan: The 40th president was shot by John Hinckley Jr. outside a Washington, D.C., hotel in March 1981. Hinckley fired his .22 revolver six times (a Secret Service agent, a D.C. policeman, and the president's press secretary were all injured). Reagan was hit in the right lung by a bullet that ricocheted off the presidential limousine. The 70-year-old recovered fully from the incident, as did two of the injured men. Press secretary James Brady was left seriously disabled by his injuries and later became a gun control advocate. Hinckley, who claimed to act to win the affection of actress Jodie Foster, was found not guilty by reason of insanity and confined to a D.C. hospital, where he remains to this day.

Ten Books Every American Should Read

Most of us read for entertainment, but American thought has long been shaped by powerful works of fiction and nonfiction that help illuminate national issues and concerns. Here are ten classic works that helped shape a nation.

1. **Common Sense (1776)**

   In language simple enough for everyone to understand, Thomas Paine's pamphlet made a case that the colonies should break with Great Britain. It was so well received that it became a best seller of sorts in its day.

2. **The Federalist Papers (1788)**

   Though the U.S. Constitution was conceived and written during the summer of 1787, the document still had to be ratified by 9 of the 13 states before it could take effect. These 85 essays, written by Alexander Hamilton, James Madison, and John Jay, implored Americans to embrace and accept the Constitution, lest the young nation fall apart.

3. **Uncle Tom's Cabin (1852)**

   Harriet Beecher Stowe's controversial novel about slavery in America became a best seller in its time and was a major factor in the development of antislavery sentiment. When Abraham Lincoln met its author, he hailed her as the little lady who started a war. The book's legacy has suffered in recent years because of its stereotypical portrayal of blacks.

4. **Adventures of Huckleberry Finn (1885)**

   Mark Twain's follow-up to *The Adventures of Tom Sawyer* is hailed by many critics and writers as the first great American novel. Twain chronicles the adventures of a young boy named Huck and his friend, a runaway slave named Jim, as they flee south along the Mississippi River. The lessons of this controversial book are undermined, some say, by its frequent use of the "n-word," and for decades it has been the target of censorship in schools and libraries.

5. **Gone with the Wind (1936)**

   Margaret Mitchell's epic romance novel brought Scarlett, Rhett, and Tara to the world, won a Pulitzer Prize, became a best seller, and was adapted to become one of the highest-grossing movies of all time. Its depictions of the Civil War and slavery have its critics, but its romantic depiction of plantation life and Southern belles has made it one of the most beloved books of all time, with more than 30 million copies sold.

6. **The Grapes of Wrath (1939)**

   John Steinbeck's story about a displaced Oklahoma family forced to abandon their farm and seek work as migrant workers during the Dust Bowl phenomenon of the early 1930s won the author a Pulitzer Prize. The book focused attention on the plight of millions of Americans suffering during the Great Depression.

7. **Invisible Man (1952)**

   Ralph Ellison's invisible man is not the victim of a freak science experiment but an African American man whose existence goes largely unseen by the larger white culture. By the end of this 600-page novel, the reader still has not learned the main character's name.

8. **Catch-22 (1961)**

   We all know war is hell, but Joseph Heller's book showed us that war could also be absurd. This satirical look at World War II contributed to the American lexicon the phrase *catch-22*, meaning, an illogical set of rules that stymie well-meaning people at every turn.

9. **Silent Spring (1962)**

   Rachel Carson's unflinching nonfiction examination of how pesticides have polluted our world is credited with sparking the birth of the environmental movement in the United States.

10. **Bury My Heart at Wounded Knee (1970)**

    Dee Brown's book examines the history of the United States through the eyes of Native Americans, paying special attention to their mistreatment at the hands of European Americans. The title of this controversial best seller refers to the massacre that took place near Wounded Knee Creek, South Dakota. There, in 1890, more than 150 Lakota Sioux were killed by the 7th Cavalry in what is considered the last major armed confrontation between Indians and U.S. government officials.

Who was Geronimo and why do we yell his name when we jump?

Geronimo was the nickname of a fierce Apache warrior who fought in the Apache Wars, which occurred from about 1849 to 1886 in the American Southwest. The Apaches fought to keep their land from invaders such as the neighboring Mexicans and white American newcomers. It's rumored that Geronimo got his nickname from his Mexican adversaries, who allegedly screamed for mercy to St. Jerome, a patron saint, as the Native American warrior attacked them. After a lifetime of battles, Geronimo surrendered to the U.S. Army and spent the rest of his life as a prisoner of war. He died of pneumonia in 1909. A mere three years later, Hollywood featured his character and likeness in various westerns—some good, mostly bad.

A 1939 version of his life story—which, according to the movie trailers, promised to titillate viewers with the tale of this "war-mad demon"—was shown one night at the movie theater in Fort Benning, Georgia, that had become a training ground for the first crop of American paratroopers. Leaping from aircraft with a parachute was a new endeavor for soldiers, and the drills were nerve-wracking. After watching the film, a private from Georgia named Aubrey Eberhardt allegedly boasted to his compatriots that the next day he would scream "Geronimo!" as he jumped from the plane. That way, everyone would know he was as fearless as the Indian warrior. Eberhardt lived up to his promise, and his buddies did the same.

Though not officially sanctioned, the rallying cry spread throughout the U.S. military. Today, American children know they are supposed to yell "Geronimo!" at the tops of their lungs, even when leaping from heights no taller than a jungle gym.

The irony is, Geronimo was not the great warrior's real name. It was Goyathlay, a name that means "one who yawns." But that would hardly make for an impressive war cry, now would it?

Some U.S. Currency Worth Keeping

An 1804 silver dollar is worth about $10 million, but you probably won't find one in your pocket change. In fact, most of the coins that pass through your hands are unlikely to be valuable. But surprises are always possible. That's why it's worth getting a wholesale guidebook to coin values (known as "The Official Blue Book") and occasionally checking currency to see what dealers would pay for it.

Things to keep in mind: (1) The better a bill or coin looks, the more collectors want it. In general, heavily circulated coins are tarnished, worn out, or damaged, so they don't fetch a high price. Uncirculated coins are worth more, especially if they bear a key date. The same goes for crisp banknotes. (2) Older is not always better. Many modern coins were minted with errors that make them valuable. (3) Resist the urge to clean coins or iron bills. You could be doing more harm than good.

The following are some numismatic items to be on the lookout for.

Indian Head Pennies and Wheat Cents

Indian head pennies are so hard to find in spare change nowadays that they're worth keeping when you do come across one, even if they aren't worth much. Those minted before 1880 are more valuable. From 1909 to 1958, the back of the Lincoln penny showed two stalks of wheat. Though these coins are old, they are also plentiful and usually worn. Nice specimens are worth a few times their face value.

Buffalo Nickels

These are nice to find and fun to keep but not valuable unless they're in perfect condition. (The dates tend to wear off quickly.) An exception is the 1937-D, which appears to show a three-legged buffalo on the back. If you find this, it's worth having it appraised.

State Quarters

Beginning in 1999, the U.S. Mint began releasing quarters commemorating each of the 50 states. The 2004-D Wisconsin quarter and 2001-P New York quarter are known to have errors, so they are worth inspecting carefully. The New York error is obvious: the coin was struck twice. The Wisconsin error is subtle: an extra leaf was added to an ear of corn in its reverse. In addition, coin shops are always on the lookout for entire rolls of quarters for specific states and may pay you more than face value for them.

"Junk Silver" Coins

Some coins are valuable for the metal they contain. Kennedy half dollars, Roosevelt dimes, and Washington quarters struck before 1965 are most valuable. An extremely rare 1965 Roosevelt dime made with silver is worth thousands.

Presidential Dollars

These new gold-colored dollar coins are leaving U.S. Mints with so many mistakes that they are worth a careful inspection. One common error: the edges of the coins are missing their inscriptions, which say, among other things, *E pluribus unum*, the Latin phrase meaning, "Out of many, one."

$2 Bills

The Jefferson bills that were released between 1929 and 1966 occasionally turn up; they're fun to collect even if they're so beat up they aren't worth much. As for $2 bills released in 1976 and later, spend 'em.

Why is the UN in the USA?

Technically, it's not. Although the United Nations headquarters occupies 18 acres in New York City, by international agreement that parcel of land is treated as though it is not a part of the United States. Federal, state, and local authorities cannot enter the property without permission of the UN's secretary-general.

The United Nations is sited in the United States because the American government played an enormous role in conceiving, promoting, and bankrolling this international organization. The term *United Nations* was first conceived by President Franklin D. Roosevelt and trotted out in 1942, when a group of countries agreed they would fight the aggressors of World War II. In the spring of 1945, before the war had even ended, 50 nations signed a charter to promote world peace. Later that year, when the war was over, the UN seemed like a good idea, for all nations knew they could not risk another global conflict.

Not surprisingly, it was the victors of World War II—the United States, Britain, France, the Soviet Union, and the Republic of China—who became the main players in the creation of the United Nations. In 1945, when the first UN meetings were conducted, Europe was still in a state of devastation. Therefore, situating the headquarters in the United States may have seemed like a smart decision. The UK, France, and the Netherlands voted against the decision, but the United States controlled the vote by virtue of its clout and willingness to bankroll the fledgling organization. (To this day, the United States continues to exert strong veto power over UN actions and budgets.) Canada was considered briefly, as were other cities throughout the United States. The matter was settled when the Rockefeller family bought land in uptown Manhattan for $8.5 million and donated it to the UN. An international committee of architects designed the ultramodern complex.

For the record, other significant UN buildings are located all over the world. And, from time to time, there's talk of moving the headquarters out of New York. Nothing's come of it yet.

Why do we have fireworks on the Fourth of July?

Fireworks are not a uniquely American form of entertainment, nor are they exclusive to the nation's July Fourth revelry. Gunpowder-filled pyrotechnics were invented by the Chinese more than 1,300 years ago. Later they were imported to Europe, probably during the time of the Crusades, giving people a way to extend celebrations into the nighttime hours. Early American colonists brought fireworks to North America and used them well before the Revolutionary War.

The most famous mention of Independence Day fireworks was penned by John Adams, one of the Founding Fathers. In a letter to his wife, Abigail, written the day after colonists broke with their king, Adams predicted that Americans would forever mark the occasion in a big way. Notice, though, that he referred to the nation's "true" birthday: "The second day of July, 1776, will be memorable epoch in the history of America," he wrote. "I am apt to believe that it will be celebrated by succeeding generations, as the great Anniversary Festival. It ought to be commemorated, as the day of deliverance by solemn acts of devotion to God Almighty. It ought to be solemnized with pomp, shows, games, sports, guns, bells, bonfires and illuminations, from one end of the continent to the other, from this time forward forever."

Fireworks became associated with major events, such as the day George Washington became president. After a long day in April 1789, people celebrated his swearing-in with a parade and late-night fireworks in New York City, the nation's first capital.

Ten Fun Facts about the Statue of Liberty

1. Given to the United States by France in 1886, the Statue of Liberty was meant to commemorate the friendship between the two countries established during the American Revolution.

2. Sculptor Frédéric Auguste Bartholdi designed the Statue. It's said that he modeled Lady Liberty's face after his mother.

3. The Statue is 305 feet and 1 inch from the base of the pedestal to the tip of the flame.

4. Total weight is 450,000 pounds.

5. The Statue is made of copper 3/32 inch thick, the same thickness as two pennies put together.

6. Viewing decks are located on the pedestal and crown. Many people who have visited think they have been inside the torch, but that area has been closed to the public since an explosion on July 30, 1916.

7. The torch is a symbol of enlightenment. The Statue of Liberty's torch lights the way to freedom, showing us the path to liberty.

8. In her left hand, the statue holds a tablet bearing the date of the United States' independence, July 4, 1776, written in Roman numerals (July IV, MDCCLXXVI).

9. The seven spikes on her crown represent the seas and continents of the world.

10. The Statue of Liberty is on Liberty Island. Administered by the National Park Service, the property is located within the territorial jurisdiction of the state of New York.

How to Grill the Perfect Hamburger

Nothing's more American than a juicy burger with all the fixings. Some burgers are so good they make you want to wave Old Glory. Others remind you of Canada and hockey: too much puck. The perfect patty starts with the right ingredients and calls for flawless, near-scientific execution. Here's how to make your country proud.

1. **Buy the right meat.** You want ground chuck not ground beef. The former means the meat comes from a single part of the animal; the latter is a hodgepodge of unspecified bits. Choose meat that is 70 to 80 percent lean. This means it is also 20 to 30 percent fat. Fat is flavor. Fat is juicy. If you are buying from a premium

butcher shop, ask for twice-ground chuck. The burgers will form better.

2. **Build a better patty.** Aim for a six-ounce burger. A quarter pound is a tad skimpy; a half pound unwieldy. Avoid adding onions, condiments, and other extras to the meat; they obscure flavor and make the burger fall apart. Handle the meat as little as possible. Use only the amount you need to form a patty; use a kitchen scale to gauge the correct weight. Roll the meat into a ball between your palms and then flatten it. Shoot for 1/2 inch to 3/4 inch thick. Gently dent the top of the burger with your thumb to keep it from turning into a balloon when it's cooked.

3. **Fire up the grill.** Use an outdoor grill, and don't even think of cooking burgers until the coals are beginning to redden and the grill is so hot you can't hover your hand over it. Brush the grill lightly with

olive or vegetable oil. Sprinkle the burgers with salt and pepper and lay them on the grill for 3 to 4 minutes. Wait patiently and then flip and cook for another 3 to 4 minutes. Never press the patties with a spatula, which only squeezes out the juice. Use a meat thermometer to tell if they're ready. It is recommended that you cook ground beef to between 160°F and 165°F. The former temperature tends to yield a medium-rare burger; the latter a medium burger. If you must cook indoors, use a cast-iron skillet with a raised bottom that keeps the patty above the grease. And make sure you have plenty of ventilation.

4. **Work the follow-through.** All the accompanying ingredients should match the quality of the meat. If you're using cheese, it should be thin and sturdy enough to melt on the burger. Place it on the patty close to completion of cooking. Bacon should

be prepared ahead of time and served grease-free and at room temperature. Buns should be warm, whether grilled outdoors or heated in the oven. Offer guests a selection of high-quality condiments and fresh vegetables (onions, lettuce, tomatoes, etc.). Assemble burgers as soon as they come off the grill. Perfection!

How to Fold an American Flag

This symbolic act is harder than it looks. U.S. flags are traditionally folded into a shape that's reminiscent of a tri-corn hat (typically worn by men during the Revolutionary War). Two people are required to properly fold a flag. If you've never done it before, you and your partner might want to practice privately to avoid embarrassing slipups. The big rule: At no time should the flag touch the ground. Your movements must be crisp and sure. Both folders must maintain a firm grip on the flag throughout to ensure that the ends don't flop free.

1. Start by folding the flag in half. The blue field with stars—called the union—should be on the outside.

2. Fold the flag in half again, keeping the union to the outside.

3. The person holding the striped end of the flag begins a series of triangular folds in the direction of the union. With large, ceremonial flags, you should make 12 folds before reaching the union.

4. Now the person holding the striped end holds the folded flag while the person holding the union end makes the 13th and final fold—symbolizing the 13 original states—and tucks this triangular flap snugly into the opening.

5. The result is a tidy triangular shape. If the flag will be used again, unfold it by reversing each of these steps.

"The Star-Spangled Banner" by Francis Scott Key

The red rockets and bursting bombs in the U.S. national anthem may seem to symbolize adversity, metaphorical or otherwise. But the lyrics of "The Star-Spangled Banner" refer specifically to the Battle of Fort McHenry, during the War of 1812. This was the first war declared by the United States after the American Revolution, and once again the opponent was Great Britain.

In September 1814, as the battle raged on, a lawyer named Francis Scott Key approached a group of British officers to negotiate the release of American prisoners. Unfortunately, Key boarded the HMS *Tonnant* just as the British fleet was preparing to attack Fort McHenry,

Baltimore harbor's defense against invasion. Once the negotiations were complete, the Brits refused to let him and his companions leave; they had no intention of letting the men blab news of the impending attack to their fellow Americans.

So Key was forced to watch the event from the British ship. The next morning, when the smoke cleared, Key spied the 15-star, 15-stripe American flag still flying over the fort. The flag said it all: the Americans had triumphed. Inspired by the scene, Key composed a poem describing his experience, which he wrote on the back of an envelope.

It quickly became popular with Americans. Despite the wartime references, the poem was set to music and performed during countless civic and sporting events. It wasn't until 1931 that Congress and President Herbert Hoover made it the official national anthem. The poem and song consist of four stanzas, but the first—wherein Key describes his elation upon seeing the flag—is the one that is sung most often. The anthem was not the young lawyer's only gift to his country: a phrase found in the last stanza became the nation's motto (albeit paraphrased) in 1956: In God We Trust.

The original Star-Spangled Banner was carefully preserved and is now the jewel of the Smithsonian's American history collection. Here are Key's now-famous words:

> *Oh, say can you see by the dawn's early light*
> *What so proudly we hailed at the twilight's last gleaming?*
> *Whose broad stripes and bright stars thru the perilous fight,*
> *O'er the ramparts we watched were so gallantly streaming?*
> *And the rocket's red glare, the bombs bursting in air,*

Gave proof through the night that
our flag was still there.

Oh, say does that star-spangled
banner yet wave

O'er the land of the free and the
home of the brave?

On the shore, dimly seen through the
mists of the deep,

Where the foe's haughty host in dread
silence reposes,

What is that which the breeze, o'er
the towering steep,

As it fitfully blows, half conceals,
half discloses?

Now it catches the gleam of the
morning's first beam,

In full glory reflected now shines in
the stream:

'Tis the star-spangled banner! Oh
long may it wave

O'er the land of the free and the home of the brave!

And where is that band who so vauntingly swore

That the havoc of war and the battle's confusion,

A home and a country should leave us no more!

Their blood has washed out their foul footsteps' pollution.

No refuge could save the hireling and slave

From the terror of flight, or the gloom of the grave:

And the star-spangled banner in triumph doth wave

O'er the land of the free and the home of the brave!

Oh! thus be it ever, when freemen shall stand

Between their loved home and the war's desolation!

Blest with victory and peace, may the heav'n rescued land

Praise the Power that hath made and preserved us a nation.

Then conquer we must, when our cause it is just,

And this be our motto: "In God is our trust."

And the star-spangled banner in triumph shall wave

O'er the land of the free and the home of the brave!

The Pledge of Allegiance

The Pledge of Allegiance was written in August 1892 by Francis Bellamy and was first published in *The Youth's Companion* on September 8, 1892. Originally, Bellamy had written the pledge so that it could be used by citizens in any country. However, in 1923, the words "the flag of the United States of America" were added.

In 1954, President Eisenhower encouraged Congress to add "under God" to the pledge. These two words have caused a lot of kerfuffle, culminating in legal battles that ended up in the U.S. Supreme Court. Those who support the words' inclusion cite that the phrase has been in the pledge for more than 50 years and that this country was founded based on religious beliefs; opponents argue for a separation of church and state. As of today, the pledge reads:

> *I pledge allegiance to the flag of the United States of America, and to the republic for which it stands, one nation under God, indivisible, with liberty and justice for all.*

Each morning, children in schoolrooms across America stand and pledge allegiance to the flag. When pledging allegiance, you should be standing at attention facing the flag, with your right hand over your heart. Those in military uniform remain silent during the recitation of the pledge, face the flag, and render the military salute.

What is the electoral college?

Every four years, when Americans vote for a president, they are participating in a popular, or people-based, election. Yet, according to the U.S. Constitution, the president is not elected by popular vote. That responsibility falls to the members of the mysterious electoral college. You probably learned about this entity in tenth-grade social studies class, but, if you're like most people, you've forgotten what it actually does.

When the framers of the Constitution were hammering out the details in the summer of 1787, they worried that ordinary people would lack the intelligence and know-how to properly elect a president. This fear wasn't as condescending as it might seem. Remember, the new nation was big. It took weeks and sometimes months for news to travel. The framers didn't think it was possible for voters, even if they were educated, to know everything necessary about all the candidates. In a vast governmental system of checks and balances, the electoral college seemed like a good way to guard against an uninformed decision by the people.

The system, established in Article II, Section 1 of the Constitution, has evolved slightly over the years. Today there are 538 electoral votes distributed among the 50 states and the District of Columbia. In 48 states, whoever wins the popular vote gets *all* of that state's electoral votes. (Maine and Nebraska have slightly different rules.)

The process for choosing electors varies. Electors can be political party stalwarts who are nominated to a state's ballot as a reward for their work. They are elected by voters on Election Day and then meet in their state's capital in December of a presidential election year to officially cast their votes. Technically, electors can go off-script and vote for a candidate other than the one they pledged to vote for, but that hardly ever happens.

If you think the electoral college sounds strange, join the club. Many critiques have been leveled at the system in the last 220-plus years. At least four times in history, disputes over the electoral votes have led to a messy presidential election.

The most recent: the Bush–Gore election of 2000. Gore won the popular vote by about 500 votes. But the race was so tight in Florida that the two candidates ended up duking it out over that state's electoral votes all the way to the Supreme Court.

Regardless of such problems, it's unlikely the electoral college will go away anytime soon. You need a two-thirds vote of Congress and three-fourths ratification by the states to pass a Constitutional amendment. That's tough to do without huge national consensus. Apparently, as much as Americans love complaining about the electoral college, they like adding up to 270 on election night even more.

What's a bicameral congress?

icameral simply means "two houses" and refers to the Senate and the House of Representatives. During the Constitutional Convention of 1787, the framers of the Constitution debated how the large and small states would best be represented in Congress. Ultimately, they arrived at the Great Compromise: a state's population would determine how many representatives it would have in the House of Representatives, and all states would have the same number of senators (two). Representatives are elected for a two-year term, which is why they always seem to be in perpetual reelection mode. By contrast, the members of the more "prestigious" Senate are elected for six-year terms.

Can anyone run for president?

Pretty much. To qualify for the U.S. House of Representatives, you must be at least 25 years old, a U.S. citizen for at least seven years, and a resident of the state you're hoping to represent. To run for senator, you must be at least 30 years old, a U.S. citizen for at least nine years, and a resident of the state that elects you. (That is, you can't run for senator of Nebraska while living in Alaska.) Technically, you can campaign for and even be elected to either the Senate or the House of Representatives without meeting the age and citizenship requirements, as long as you reach the targets before being sworn in.

The qualifications for president are much stricter. You must be at least 35 years old. You must have lived in the United States for at least

14 years. And you must be a "natural-born citizen" of the United States. The phrasing of this last qualification has never been interpreted by the Supreme Court. A naturalized citizen *could* become a senator or representative but never president. In a worst-case scenario, in which a naturalized member of congress or cabinet member (such as Henry Kissinger or Madeline Albright) was next in line to become president, that person would be ineligible.

Ten Quotations That Embody the American Spirit

Although historians have questioned the accuracy of several of these quotations, they endure because they succinctly express some uniquely American ideals.

1. **"The buck stops here."**

   Harry S Truman was a humble haberdasher from Missouri who became vice president and inherited the highest office in the land after President Franklin Roosevelt died in office in 1945. A friend presented the new president with a sign emblazoned with these words, which Truman proudly displayed on his desk and referred to in speeches. It was his way of saying that blame and responsibility for big decisions always fall to the president.

2. **"Give me liberty or give me death!"**

These famous words, ascribed to Virginia orator Patrick Henry, became emblematic of the American position at the start of the Revolutionary War. If Henry did utter them—and the exact content of his speech is debated to this day—they would have been spoken during a speech to the House of Burgesses in Richmond about a month before the first shots were fired at Lexington and Concord.

3. **"A house divided against itself cannot stand."**

Originally from the New Testament, these words might appear to describe the Civil War. They were in fact spoken by Abraham Lincoln in 1858, two years before he was elected president. In one of his most famous speeches—given during an unsuccessful bid for a senate seat—Lincoln presciently warned that the issue of slavery would lead to national disharmony and could threaten to tear the states apart.

4. **"Speak softly and carry a big stick."**

Theodore Roosevelt first used this phrase while still governor of New York, but its principles—careful negotiation, backed up by military might—embodied his as well as many other presidencies well into the cold war era. Roosevelt, who ascended to the presidency after the assassination of William McKinley, was often depicted in political cartoons wielding a club.

5. **"I have a dream."**

In the summer of 1963, Dr. Martin Luther King Jr. gave his most famous speech in front of the Lincoln Memorial. He explained the desire for civil rights of all African Americans, drawing inspiration from the Declaration of Independence, the Constitution, and the Gettysburg Address. Though King wrote the speech ahead of time, he improvised its most famous words on the spot.

6. **"Ask not what your country can do for you—ask what you can do for your country."**

   John F. Kennedy uttered these words during his inauguration speech in 1961. The youngest president to be elected to the White House exhorted a nation of citizens, young and old, to patriotic service.

7. **"Go West, young man."**

   This phrase has been long attributed to Horace Greeley, a 19th-century New York newspaper editor. Though the phrase's origins are still debated, it expresses the notion of Manifest Destiny, the idea that the United States was destined to be settled from coast to coast by young Americans in search of opportunity.

8. **"A penny saved is a penny earned."**

Ben Franklin actually wrote, "A penny saved is twopence dear." Either way, his maxim on frugality speaks to the core of the American dream: if you work hard and are frugal, you can amass a fortune.

9. **"Well-behaved women seldom make history."**

This witty line was penned by Harvard historian Louise Thatcher Ulrich in her first academic article as a young graduate student in 1976. Though she was referring to the lives of Puritan women, the sentence caught on and became a rallying cry for the women's movement; it appeared on T-shirts, coffee mugs, and bumper stickers throughout the country. In 2007, Ulrich published a book about women in history that uses her now-famous sentence as the title.

10. "I have not yet begun to fight!"

U.S. naval captain John Paul Jones, a short but scrappy Scotsman, uttered these words during a brutal sea battle against a British frigate during the Revolutionary War. Though his ship, the *Bonhomme Richard*, was burning and taking on water, Jones stubbornly refused to surrender. Luckily, the battle turned and the Brits surrendered to Jones shortly thereafter. His words embody both American stubbornness and bravery—the willingness to fight for, and the idealist refusal to give up on, what you believe in.

Who played the first game of baseball?

That depends on whom you ask. It seems that an early version of baseball appeared in England in the 18th century and evolved side-by-side with cricket and other stick-and-ball games. *The Oxford English Dictionary* claims that the word *baseball* first appeared in Jane Austen's book *Northanger Abbey*, published in 1796. But nearly 20 years earlier, during the Revolutionary War, a young officer in George Washington's army recorded that soldiers at Valley Forge "playd at base" to kill time.

These early games were played by kids, families, hobbyists, and other amateurs using rules concocted on the fly. The first game using official rules took place June 19, 1846. On that day, the New York Nine trounced the New York Knickerbockers, 23–1 on a field in Hoboken, New Jersey, just across the Hudson River from New York City. The game was governed by the Knickerbocker (or Cartwright) Rules, which later evolved into the official rules used today. But the players of that particular game were amateurs who paid membership dues to their respective clubs in order to participate.

The first professional-league game was played on May 4, 1871, in Fort Wayne, Indiana, under the auspices of the National Association of Professional Base Ball Players. In that game, the Fort Wayne Kekiongas beat the Cleveland Forest Cities, 2–0. The first true major league game—with professional, paid players—occurred on April 22, 1876, when the Boston Red Stockings (which later morphed into the Atlanta Braves) crushed the Philadelphia Athletics, 6–5. The game took place at Jefferson Street Grounds in Philadelphia.

How to Bake the Perfect Apple Pie

A s American as apple pie!" Now that's a saying that shows you just how much the classic dessert has become an icon for an entire country. English, Dutch, and Swedish recipes for apple pie date back centuries, but Americans perfected the apple pie and made it their own. This no-fail recipe is a homerun with guests every time. Serve it at your next Fourth of July picnic.

1/2 cup white sugar
1/2 cup brown sugar
2 tablespoons all-purpose flour
1/2 teaspoon ground cinnamon
1/4 teaspoon ground nutmeg
7 cups peeled and sliced Granny Smith apples
1 recipe pastry for a 9-inch double-crust pie

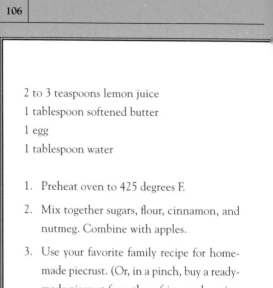

2 to 3 teaspoons lemon juice
1 tablespoon softened butter
1 egg
1 tablespoon water

1. Preheat oven to 425 degrees F.

2. Mix together sugars, flour, cinnamon, and nutmeg. Combine with apples.

3. Use your favorite family recipe for home-made piecrust. (Or, in a pinch, buy a ready-made piecrust from the refrigerated section of your grocery store.) Line a 9-inch deep-dish pie pan with one crust.

4. Pour apple mixture into crust. Sprinkle with lemon juice and dot with butter.

5. Cut the second crust into strips and weave to form a latticework over the top of the filled pie. Crimp edges.

6. Make an egg wash by whisking together

the egg and water. Brush top of crust with egg wash.

7. Bake pie for 40 to 50 minutes until fruit is tender and crust is browned. If edges are browning too quickly, cover edges with strips of foil.

8. Let pie cool a couple of hours before serving. Serve plain or with vanilla ice cream or whipped cream. Apple pie is great for breakfast the next day, too.

Why do we pay income tax to the government?

ecause the Constitution allows the government to collect it—sort of.

In the days before the Constitution was drafted, the fledgling nation was governed by a document called the Articles of Confederation, which did not give the federal government the power to tax. If the feds needed money, they had to ask the states nicely, and maybe, just maybe, the states would send them a fraction of the requested amount. American citizens liked this system, because no one likes to pay taxes. But without taxes, the nation was in trouble. For example, the government was unable to raise an army or a navy, and the country was vulnerable to attack from the British,

French, and Spanish who still maintained forts in or near the United States.

When they wrote the Constitution, the framers specifically gave Congress the power to tax and spend. They just didn't give them the right to tax people's incomes. If Congress levied a tax, it had to be levied across the board, on *all* citizens, throughout a state. They couldn't single out one person and demand payment just from him.

Then came a war. To pay for the Civil War, the feds instituted a temporary 3 percent tax on the income of the nation's richest Americans. This was hardly popular, but once Uncle Sam got a taste, he couldn't go back. He tried it again in 1894. In 1895, the Supreme Court slapped Uncle Sam, saying that if the government wanted to tax a person's individual property, it had to do so in the time-honored way: across the board, through the states. This was impossible to do, so the feds dropped the issue.

In 1913, the feds and states ratified the 16th Amendment, which gave Congress the right to tax personal income. Though the amendment has been challenged by tax protestors, it remains in effect. It's the reason the Internal Revenue Service exists, and the reason for the annual pain Americans feel emanating from their checkbooks.

What's the difference between the FBI, the CIA, and the NSA?

There are more acronymic U.S. agencies than you probably ever need to know, and all of them behave as if they are safeguarding top-secret information. But these three are in a league of their own. Each is charged with protecting a slightly different piece of the American pie.

The **Federal Bureau of Investigation** is a law enforcement agency in charge of investigating interstate criminal activities. The minute a criminal crosses state lines in the commission of a crime, he triggers a federal investigation. Kidnapping, mail fraud, bank fraud, drug trafficking, white-collar crime, terrorist plots, violent crime, illegal gambling, racketeering—all are the domain of the FBI.

The **Central Intelligence Agency** is a civilian agency tasked with collecting information from foreign sources—people, corporations, or governments—that could potentially impact the safety and welfare of U.S. citizens. The agency collects information covertly in the field, and although its employees are not a part of the U.S. military, the CIA can use military personnel to conduct covert intelligence-gathering operations.

The **National Security Agency** is the nation's top eavesdropping and code-breaking agency. It's charged with keeping criminals and spies from hacking into critical U.S. databases and stealing vital intelligence. It also monitors "signals" from various communication streams around the world, determining which are vital for U.S. national security, and then passes that data along to the appropriate agency. Good luck getting more specific information than this. The NSA is the most secretive of all U.S. agencies.

Does the Secret Service protect anything besides the president?

Yes. The Secret Service is tasked with protecting two things: people and money. The people include not just the current president but also visiting dignitaries and occasionally presidential candidates. They also investigate counterfeiting and work to ensure that banking payment systems function flawlessly and without interruption.

Can I really write a check on anything?

Yes, but you won't get too far with it. Technically, as long as a check contains essential information (your signature, the name of the person you're paying, the amount of money, the name of your bank, the date, and the phrase *pay to the order of*), it can be written on anything—a napkin, a scrap of paper, a pair of boxer shorts. Even those giant cardboard checks presented to charities and sweepstakes winners on TV are negotiable. The catch is that no one, from supermarket clerks to IRS agents, is under any obligation to accept your handmade banking instrument. In fact, computerization and modern banking procedures have made it increasingly difficult to pass a check that does not look like most other checks. The fine print in most bank account agreements spell out that customers must use "approved" checks. ATM machines make it hard to deposit checks that aren't printed on paper and conform to the conventional size and design. And the Check 21 Act of 2003, which allows banks to make digital copies of checks for easier processing, ensures that most bank tellers would reject any version that cannot be scanned digitally.

Ten Things You Can Make with a Bandana

The classic bandana was a handy tool for the cowboys of the American West. On long cattle drives, it could be tied around the neck to protect skin from sunburn or wrapped across the nose and mouth to keep out dust. But the usefulness of the bandana didn't end there. Here are ten more uses from days gone by.

1. **Coffee filter:** Boil coffee straight in a pot set on a campfire. Pour the pot's contents through the bandana and into a waiting mug.

2. **Washcloth:** Next time you have to bathe in a stream, bring along a bar of soap and a bandana.

3. **Valuables holder:** Place spectacles, jewelry, and letters from your sweet mama into the center of a bandana. Fold up the corners or roll the bandana until it cradles your treasures snugly. Tuck the precious bundle in a shirt pocket, duster, or saddlebag.

4. **Pot holder:** Before reaching for that coffeepot or skillet from the campfire, fold a bandana twice and use it to shield your hand from the hot handle.

5. **Bandage, sling, or tourniquet:** Got yourself bit by a rattler? Steer gored you? Sprained a wrist roping? Don't go crying for a first-aid kit. Patch yourself up with a bandana until the doc arrives.

6. **Flag or signal:** Sometimes you need to wave down your fellow cowpokes from a great distance away. Nothing better than a bandana for this task, whether it's flapped from your hand or tied to a pole.

A couple of them tied to tree branches make handy trail markers as well.

7. **Slingshot:** Place a rock in the middle of a bandana. Firmly grab the two corners of its right side between your thumb and first two fingers. Grab the two corners of its left side between your ring finger and pinkie. The rock should hang in a pouch. Swing the pouch over your head to pick up speed. When the rock's swinging good and fast, release the two corners held by your ring and pinkie finger and let the rock sail toward its target. With practice you'll nail those jackrabbits.

8. **Bindlestiff:** Place all your worldly possessions into a large bandana. Lay a carrying stick lightly on top of the mess of items. Carefully draw up two opposite corners of the bandana and tie them to each other above the stick. Tie the remaining two ends of the bandana over the stick.

Grasp the stick and carry it, bundle and all, over your shoulder.

9. **Lens cleaner:** Pack one bandana away from the elements to keep it relatively dust- and grit-free for the next time you need to clean your binoculars or eyeglasses.

10. **Toilet paper:** As a last resort, when nothing's handy. Another good reason to pack multiple bandanas.

Abraham Lincoln's "Gettysburg Address"

It's only 10 sentences and 272 words long, but this remarkably concise speech brilliantly summarizes the essence of what it means to be American. Ostensibly, President Abraham Lincoln was trying to explain why the United States was fighting the Civil War. But his words encompass so many sacred American touchstones—the Revolutionary War, the right of all humans to be equal, government by the people, self-sacrifice, freedom, and the notion that strength comes from unity—that it has become the nation's most beloved speech.

Gettysburg was the bloodiest battle of the Civil War. In July 1863, over the course of three days, 50,000 people lost their lives. Though the war would rage on for another two years, Gettysburg residents paid tribute to soldiers on both sides of the conflict by dedicating a cemetery to their memory. In late November of that same year, 15,000 people gathered for the dedication. Lincoln was not the featured speaker. That honor went to a famous orator who rattled on for two hours. Then Lincoln delivered a two-minute speech he'd started writing in Washington, D.C., and finished in Pennsylvania. His genius was to use simple, powerful language that harkened not to the Constitution but to the Declaration of Independence as the source of all American ideals. The words of the address are engraved into the south wall of the Lincoln Memorial.

Four score and seven years ago our fathers brought forth on this continent a new nation, conceived in liberty, and dedicated to the proposition that all men are created equal. Now we are engaged in a great civil war, testing whether that nation, or any nation, so conceived and so dedicated, can long endure. We are

met on a great battle-field of that war.
We have come to dedicate a portion of
that field, as a final resting place for
those who here gave their lives that that
nation might live. It is altogether fitting
and proper that we should do this.

But, in a larger sense, we can not
dedicate, we can not consecrate, we can
not hallow this ground. The brave men,
living and dead, who struggled here,
have consecrated it, far above our poor
power to add or detract. The world will
little note, nor long remember what we
say here, but it can never forget what
they did here.

It is for us the living, rather, to be
dedicated here to the unfinished work
which they who fought here have thus
far so nobly advanced. It is rather for
us to be here dedicated to the great task
remaining before us—that from these
honored dead we take increased devotion

to that cause for which they gave the last full measure of devotion—that we here highly resolve that these dead shall not have died in vain—that this nation, under God, shall have a new birth of freedom—and that government of the people, by the people, for the people, shall not perish from the earth.

The Declaration of Independence

One of the two most important documents in the founding of the United States, the Declaration of Independence contains many famous phrases every American should know. Here is the text of that seminal document.

In Congress, July 4, 1776

The unanimous Declaration of the thirteen united States of America

When in the Course of human events it becomes necessary for one people to dissolve the political bands which have connected them with another and to assume among the powers of the earth, the separate and equal station to which the Laws of Nature and of Nature's God entitle them, a decent respect to the opinions of mankind requires that they should declare the causes which impel them to the separation.

We hold these truths to be self-evident, that all men are created equal, that they are endowed by their Creator with certain unalienable Rights, that among these are Life, Liberty and the pursuit of Happiness. —That to secure these rights, Governments are instituted among Men, deriving their just powers from the consent of the governed, —That whenever any Form of Government becomes destructive of these ends, it is the Right of the People to alter or to abolish it, and to institute new Government, laying its foundation on such principles and organizing its powers in such form, as to them shall seem most likely to effect their Safety and Happiness. Prudence, indeed, will dictate that Governments long established should not be changed for light and transient causes; and accordingly all experience hath shewn that mankind are more disposed to suffer, while evils are sufferable than to right themselves by abolishing the forms to which they are accustomed. But when a long train of abuses and usurpations, pursuing invariably the same Object evinces a design to reduce them under absolute Despotism, it is their right, it is their duty, to throw off such Government, and to provide new Guards for their future security. —Such has been the patient sufferance of these Colonies; and such is now the necessity which constrains them to alter their former Systems of Government. The history of the present King of Great Britain is a history of repeated injuries and usurpations, all having in direct object the establishment of an absolute Tyranny over these States. To prove this, let Facts be submitted to a candid world.

He has refused his Assent to Laws, the most wholesome and necessary for the public good.

He has forbidden his Governors to pass Laws of immediate and pressing importance, unless suspended in their operation till his Assent should be obtained; and when so suspended, he has utterly neglected to attend to them.

He has refused to pass other Laws for the accommodation of large districts of people, unless those people would relinquish the right of Representation in the Legislature, a right inestimable to them and formidable to tyrants only.

He has called together legislative bodies at places unusual, uncomfortable, and distant from the depository of their Public Records, for the sole purpose of fatiguing them into compliance with his measures.

He has dissolved Representative Houses repeatedly, for opposing with manly firmness his invasions on the rights of the people.

He has refused for a long time, after such dissolutions, to cause others to be elected, whereby the Legislative Powers, incapable of Annihilation, have returned to the People at large for their exercise; the State remaining in the mean time exposed to all the dangers of invasion from without, and convulsions within.

He has endeavoured to prevent the population of these States; for that purpose obstructing the Laws for Naturalization of Foreigners; refusing to pass others to encourage their migrations hither, and raising the conditions of new Appropriations of Lands.

He has obstructed the Administration of Justice by refusing his Assent to Laws for establishing Judiciary Powers.

He has made Judges dependent on his Will alone for the tenure of their offices, and the amount and payment of their salaries.

He has erected a multitude of New Offices, and sent hither swarms of Officers to harass our people and eat out their substance.

He has kept among us, in times of peace, Standing Armies without the Consent of our legislatures.

He has affected to render the Military

independent of and superior to the Civil Power.

He has combined with others to subject us to a jurisdiction foreign to our constitution, and unacknowledged by our laws; giving his Assent to their Acts of pretended Legislation:

For quartering large bodies of armed troops among us:

For protecting them, by a mock Trial from punishment for any Murders which they should commit on the Inhabitants of these States:

For cutting off our Trade with all parts of the world:

For imposing Taxes on us without our Consent:

For depriving us in many cases, of the benefit of Trial by Jury:

For transporting us beyond Seas to be tried for pretended offences:

For abolishing the free System of English Laws in a neighbouring Province, establishing therein an Arbitrary government, and enlarging its Boundaries so as to render it at once an example and fit instrument for introducing the same absolute rule into these Colonies

For taking away our Charters, abolishing our most valuable Laws and altering fundamentally the Forms of our Governments:

For suspending our own Legislatures, and declaring themselves invested with power to legislate for us in all cases whatsoever.

He has abdicated Government here, by declaring us out of his Protection and waging War against us.

He has plundered our seas, ravaged our Coasts burnt our towns, and destroyed the lives of our people.

He is at this time transporting large Armies of foreign Mercenaries to compleat the works of death, desolation, and tyranny, already begun with circumstances of Cruelty & Perfidy scarcely paralleled in the most barbarous ages, and totally unworthy the

Head of a civilized nation.

He has constrained our fellow Citizens taken Captive on the high Seas to bear Arms against their Country, to become the executioners of their friends and Brethren, or to fall themselves by their Hands.

He has excited domestic insurrections amongst us, and has endeavoured to bring on the inhabitants of our frontiers, the merciless Indian Savages whose known rule of warfare, is an undistinguished destruction of all ages, sexes and conditions.

In every stage of these Oppressions We have Petitioned for Redress in the most humble terms: Our repeated Petitions have been answered only by repeated injury. A Prince, whose character is thus marked by every act which may define a Tyrant, is unfit to be the ruler of a free people.

Nor have We been wanting in attentions to our British brethren. We have warned them from time to time of attempts by their legislature to extend an unwarrantable jurisdiction over us. We have reminded them of the circumstances of our emigration and settlement here. We have appealed to their native justice and magnanimity, and we have conjured them by the ties of our common kindred to disavow these usurpations, which would inevitably interrupt our connections and correspondence. They too have been deaf to the voice of justice and of consanguinity. We must, therefore, acquiesce in the necessity, which denounces our Separation, and hold them, as we hold the rest of mankind, Enemies in War, in Peace Friends.

We, therefore, the Representatives of the United States of America, in General Congress, Assembled, appealing to the Supreme Judge of the world for the rectitude of our intentions, do, in the Name, and by Authority of the good People of these Colonies, solemnly publish and declare, That these United Colonies are, and of Right ought to be Free and Independent States, that they are Absolved from all Allegiance to the British Crown, and that all political connection between them and the State of Great Britain, is and ought to be totally dissolved; and that as Free and Independent States, they have full Power to levy War, conclude Peace contract Alliances, establish Commerce, and to do all other Acts and Things which Independent States may of right do. —And for the support of this Declaration, with a firm reliance on the protection of Divine Providence, we mutually pledge to each other our Lives, our Fortunes and our sacred Honor.

—John Hancock

The Signers

New Hampshire: *Josiah Bartlett, William Whipple, Matthew Thornton*

Massachusetts: *John Hancock, Samuel Adams, John Adams, Robert Treat Paine, Elbridge Gerry*

Rhode Island: *Stephen Hopkins, William Ellery*

Connecticut: *Roger Sherman, Samuel Huntington, William Williams, Oliver Wolcott*

New York: *William Floyd, Philip Livingston, Francis Lewis, Lewis Morris*

New Jersey: *Richard Stockton, John Witherspoon, Francis Hopkinson, John Hart, Abraham Clark*

Pennsylvania: *Robert Morris, Benjamin Rush, Benjamin Franklin, John Morton, George Clymer, James Smith, George Taylor, James Wilson, George Ross*

Delaware: *Caesar Rodney, George Read, Thomas McKean*

Maryland: *Samuel Chase, William Paca, Thomas Stone, Charles Carroll of Carrollton*

Virginia: *George Wythe, Richard Henry Lee, Thomas Jefferson, Benjamin Harrison, Thomas Nelson, Jr., Francis Lightfoot Lee, Carter Braxton*

North Carolina: *William Hooper, Joseph Hewes, John Penn*

South Carolina: *Edward Rutledge, Thomas Heyward, Jr., Thomas Lynch, Jr., Arthur Middleton*

Georgia: *Button Gwinnett, Lyman Hall, George Walton*

Ten Patriotic Songs about the US of A

Whether you're singing at the opening of a ball game or humming along to the tune of a marching band in a Fourth of July parade, some songs are just so American, you see stars and stripes when you hear them. Here are ten well-known, well-loved patriotic songs.

1. **"Yankee Doodle," folk song**

   This song was sung by the British before and during the Revolutionary War to make fun of the "Yankees." In typically American fashion, the colonists embraced the tune and turned it into a celebration of their defiance of the British.

2. **"Stars and Stripes Forever,"**
   John Philip Sousa

   Sousa composed this march on Christmas Day 1896. It is often played by marching bands in parades and at other patriotic celebrations. By an act of Congress, it was made the national march of the United States.

3. **"You're a Grand Old Flag,"**
   George M. Cohan

   This patriotic song, a tribute to the American flag, was written in 1906 for the musical *George Washington Jr.*

4. **"This Land Is Your Land,"**
   Woody Guthrie

   One of the most beloved patriotic songs of America, "This Land Is Your Land" was written in 1940 and published in 1945. The song had a revival in the 1960s when several members of the new folk movement, including Bob Dylan, the Kingston Trio, and Peter, Paul and Mary, recorded versions.

5. **"Battle Hymn of the Republic,"**
   Julia Ward Howe

   When Julia Howe visited a Union army camp during the American Civil War, she heard the soldiers singing "John Brown's Body." Inspired by the music, she penned the lyrics to "Battle Hymn of the Republic." The hymn first appeared in the *Atlantic Monthly* in 1862.

6. **"The Star-Spangled Banner,"**
   Francis Scott Key

   Our national anthem was written by Francis Scott Key after witnessing the British attack on Fort McHenry during the War of 1812.

7. **"My Country 'Tis of Thee,"**
Samuel F. Smith

Written by the Reverend Samuel F. Smith in 1831, this song was inspired when Smith was translating a book of German patriotic songs for his friend Lowell Mason. The song is written to the British tune of "God Save the King."

8. **"America the Beautiful,"**
Katharine Lee Bates

When Bates, a professor at Wellesley College, was visiting Colorado in 1893, she hiked to the top of Pike's Peak. The breathtaking view inspired her to write a poem memorializing the natural beauty she had seen in her journey across America. The words are most commonly set to music composed by Samuel A. Ward.

9. **"Coming to America," Neil Diamond**

Released in 1980, this song is a celebration of immigration. Diamond sang it at the Statue of Liberty rededication for its centennial celebration.

10. **"God Bless America," Irving Berlin**

Often called the country's unofficial national anthem, "God Bless America" was first written by Berlin in 1918 and then put away for 20 years. In 1938, it was sung by Kate Smith on her radio show to celebrate Armistice Day.

Official Citizenship Test

We hope you've been paying attention because now it's time to test your knowledge of U.S. history and government. To become an official citizen of the United States, a newcomer must, among other things, correctly answer 6 out of 10 questions chosen from a list of 100. The basic 100 are no walk in the park, giving rise to the observation that some new citizens are better educated about American history and government than natural-born Americans. Here's a hypothetical citizenship test that incorporates some of those official questions. How many can you answer without turning to the Internet?

Questions

1. How many amendments does the Constitution have?

2. What is the "rule of law"?

3. Name one of your state's U.S. senators.

4. Why do some states have more representatives than other states?

5. What are two Cabinet-level positions?

6. *The Federalist Papers* supported the passage of the U.S. Constitution. Name one of its authors.

7. What did Susan B. Anthony do?

8. Who was president during World War I?

9. Name one of the two longest rivers in the United States.

10. Why does the flag have 13 stripes?

Answers

1. Twenty-seven.

2. Everyone must follow the law. Leaders must obey the law. Government must obey the law. No one is above the law.

3. Answers will vary. For residents of the District of Columbia and U.S. territories, the answer is that D.C. and U.S. territories have no U.S. senators.

4. The number of state representatives is based on a state's population. Some states have more because they have more people.

5. Cabinet appointees include Secretary of Agriculture, Secretary of Commerce, Secretary of Defense, Secretary of Education, Secretary of Energy, Secretary of Health and Human Services, Secretary of Homeland Security, Secretary of Housing and Urban Development, Secretary of Interior, Secretary of State, Secretary of

Transportation, Secretary of Treasury, Secretary of Veterans' Affairs, Secretary of Labor, Attorney General.

6. James Madison, Alexander Hamilton, John Jay, or "Publius" (a pen name that served as a pseudonym for any and all of these three).

7. Fought for women's rights; fought for civil rights.

8. Woodrow Wilson.

9. Missouri River; Mississippi River.

10. There were 13 original colonies; the stripes represent those original colonies.